EDGE
BOOKS

WARRIORS OF HISTORY

GLADIATORS

by **Michael Martin**

Consultant:
Dr. Kelly Olson
Department of Classical Studies
The University of Western Ontario
London, Ontario

Capstone
press®

Mankato, Minnesota

Edge Books are published by Capstone Press,
151 Good Counsel Drive, P.O. Box 669, Mankato, Minnesota 56002.
www.capstonepress.com

Library of Congress Cataloging-in-Publication Data
Martin, Michael, 1948–
    Gladiators/by Michael Martin.
    p. cm.—(Edge Books. Warriors of History)
    Includes bibliographical references and index.
    ISBN-13: 978-0-7368-6429-9 (hardcover)
    ISBN-10: 0-7368-6429-6 (hardcover)
    1. Gladiators—Rome—Juvenile literature. I. Title. II. Series.
GV35.M27 2007
796.8—dc22   2005034929

Summary: Describes Roman gladiators, including their history, weapons, and way
of life.

Editorial Credits
Mandy Robbins, editor; Thomas Emery, designer; Kim Brown, production artist;
Jo Miller, photo researcher; Scott Thoms, photo editor

Photo Credits
Art Resource, NY/Scala, 4
The Bridgeman Art Library/© National Museums of Scotland, 8–9; Thracian
    gladiator's helmet (bronze), Roman, (1st century AD)/Museo Archeologico
    Nazionale, Naples, Italy, Giraudon, 12
Corbis/Archivo Iconografico, S.A., 24; Bettmann, 6–7, 8, 10–11, 14, 17, 26;
    Christie's Images, 18, 28–29; Stapleton Collection, 20
Cynthia Martin, cover illustration, 22 (diagram)
Getty Images Inc./Time Life Pictures/J.R. Eyerman, 23
SuperStock, 27

TABLE OF CONTENTS

CHAPTER 1

ANCIENT ROME

LEARN ABOUT

- *An ancient empire*
- *Soldiers and slaves*
- *The first gladiators*

The Roman Forum was a center of activity, where people from all parts of society could come together.

From about 500 BC until AD 500, Rome was the largest, most important city in the world. It was the birthplace of the Roman Empire. About a million people traveled its narrow, winding streets every day.

The emperor was the supreme ruler of the Roman Empire. He shared power with men who were elected to the Senate. Wealthy men were most likely to become senators. But even poor men had the right to vote. Women and slaves, however, had no rights in Rome's government.

Government buildings and religious temples stood in the Roman Forum. People gathered there to hear speeches and discuss daily issues. Gladiators were a favorite topic of conversation. These well-trained warriors battled to the death in stadiums called amphitheaters. The sand-covered floors of these stadiums were called arenas. Most Romans were thrilled by the battles that went on there.

STORAX·SERVORVM
MANGO

SLAVES OF THE EMPIRE

The Roman Empire was made up of lands conquered
by the Roman army. It included much of Europe and
parts of Africa and the Middle East. The Romans made
slaves of soldiers they defeated in battle. A man called a
lanista would buy these men and train them as gladiators.

Even the toughest gladiator often began his career facing the humiliation of the auction block.

A slave was usually a slave for life. Sometimes they could buy their freedom, but the price was high. The only slaves who could hope to earn that much money were gladiators. The best gladiators could become rich and famous. Unfortunately, their jobs often forced them to kill or be killed. Few gladiators reached the age of 30.

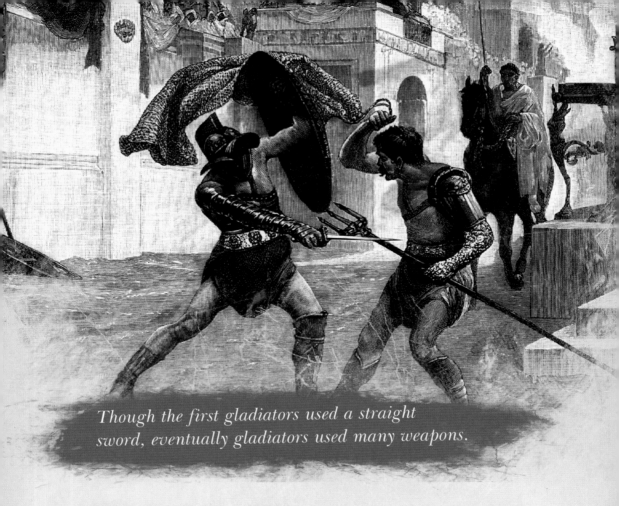

Though the first gladiators used a straight sword, eventually gladiators used many weapons.

DEADLY GAMES

In 264 BC, a man named Decimus Junius Brutus made three pairs of slaves fight to the death after his father's funeral. This match was the first recorded gladiator contest.

Fights between gladiators were called games. At first, gladiator games were limited to funerals. Soon, games were also held during Roman religious festivals. Gladiator games were so entertaining that they eventually were held at any time of the year.

At the beginning of the games, gladiators paraded into the arena wearing purple cloaks. This color was a symbol of royalty. The games themselves were held in honor of the emperor.

Most Romans enjoyed watching gladiator games. Gladiators fought in towns all over the Roman Empire. Sometimes they fought against wild animals like lions, bears, and elephants.

EDGE FACT

The first gladiators used a straight sword called a gladius. This weapon's name led to people calling the fighters gladiators.

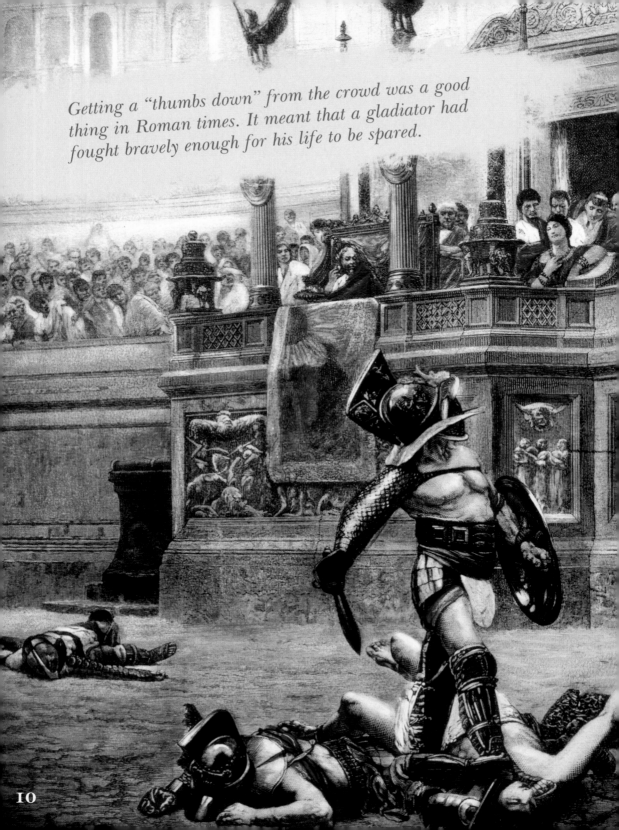

Getting a "thumbs down" from the crowd was a good thing in Roman times. It meant that a gladiator had fought bravely enough for his life to be spared.

The brutal combat between gladiators did not bother most Romans. The empire had grown powerful because its soldiers faced death with courage. Anyone who was horrified by the violence was considered weak and pitiful. Combat between gladiators was a celebration of the values that made Rome great.

CHAPTER II

LIFE AS A GLADIATOR

LEARN ABOUT
- *Gladiator schools*
- *Fighting rules*
- *Death in the arena*

Gladiator helmets have been found all over what was once the Roman Empire. The strong metal has held up for thousands of years.

Few men chose to become gladiators. Most were criminals or slaves. But some free Romans liked the idea of winning money. These people volunteered to fight. Even women fought as gladiators, although few Romans approved of women fighting. After AD 200, women were not allowed to become gladiators.

GLADIATOR TRAINING

Gladiators trained in special schools. Lanistas fed them well. Gladiators had excellent trainers, and received the best medical care.

For slaves, the schools were like prisons. These recruits could not leave. They were whipped often and lived in tiny cells.

Volunteer gladiators were treated better than slaves. They could leave the school. Some lived in the city with their families.

Gladiators trained hard so that their day in the arena wouldn't be their last.

Trainers at gladiator schools taught combat skills. Gladiators knew that each fight could be their last. They worked hard to master the skills that would keep them alive. Gladiators learned how to fight and kill with spears, daggers, and swords. They lifted weights and practiced with heavy swords to become stronger.

Gladiators spent most of their time training. They only fought two or three times a year. Gladiators learned not only how to kill, but also how to die. They were expected never to show fear.

SURVIVING THE ARENA

On the day of a contest, gladiators paraded into the arena. They began with practice fights using blunted swords. Next, they were given real weapons that had just been sharpened. Then, gladiators paired up to face opponents for a possible fight to the death.

Not every match ended in death. Referees stopped matches if there was no clear winner. In this case, both men were spared to fight another day. But if a gladiator admitted defeat, the referee called to the crowd for its decision.

EDGE FACT

It was expensive to train and feed gladiators. A lanista was not happy when one of his gladiators was killed.

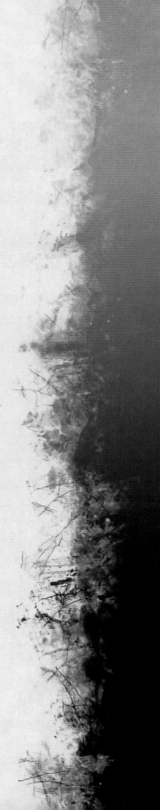

A gladiator admitted defeat by throwing down his shield and holding up a finger. If the crowd thought he had fought bravely, they gave a "thumbs down" sign. That meant the defeated gladiator's life was spared. But if the gladiator had not fought well, the people gave a "thumbs up" sign. Then, at the emperor's command, the winner plunged his weapon into the loser's neck.

BLOODY BATTLES

Gladiators were trained to make fights last as long as possible. Swords slashed at arms and legs. Spears and daggers pierced stomachs and chests. But wounds given during the match were minor. That way, the gladiators could keep fighting for the pleasure of the crowd.

Pairs of gladiators often fought in the arena at the same time. Each match was supervised by a referee.

CHAPTER III

DEADLY WEAPONS

LEARN ABOUT
- *Types of gladiators*
- *Fighting emperors*
- *Spartacus*

The retiarius was also called the fisherman because he fought with the same tools one would use to catch a fish.

Gladiators killed with swords, daggers, and spears. Some wore armor and carried shields, while others wore almost no protection. Some gladiators even fought on horseback.

SPEARS, SWORDS, NETS, AND ARMOR

Roman armies conquered many tribes throughout the world. Some gladiators used the weapons and armor of these tribes. A gladiator called a samnite wore a helmet with a crest. He fought with a sword and held a large shield. A gladiator called a retiarius wore armor only on his left arm. He carried a net and a long spear called a trident. The trident had three pointed tips. A retiarius tried to tangle his opponent in the net. After trapping his opponent, the retiarius stabbed him with the trident.

The emperor Nero was not as brave
as he wanted people to think.

FIGHTING EMPERORS

Emperors and other noblemen were not supposed to perform in public. But that didn't stop several emperors from fighting as gladiators. They couldn't resist the excitement of the arena.

Emperors usually made sure they were in little real danger. The emperor Nero, for example, faced a lion in the arena. But first, he had the lion drugged so that it could barely stand up.

The emperor Commodus was cruel and possibly insane. He fought many times as a gladiator. Commodus never lost a fight, which is not as amazing as it sounds. His opponents were forced to use wooden swords. Meanwhile, Commodus used a real sword. He particularly enjoyed slicing off opponents' ears and noses.

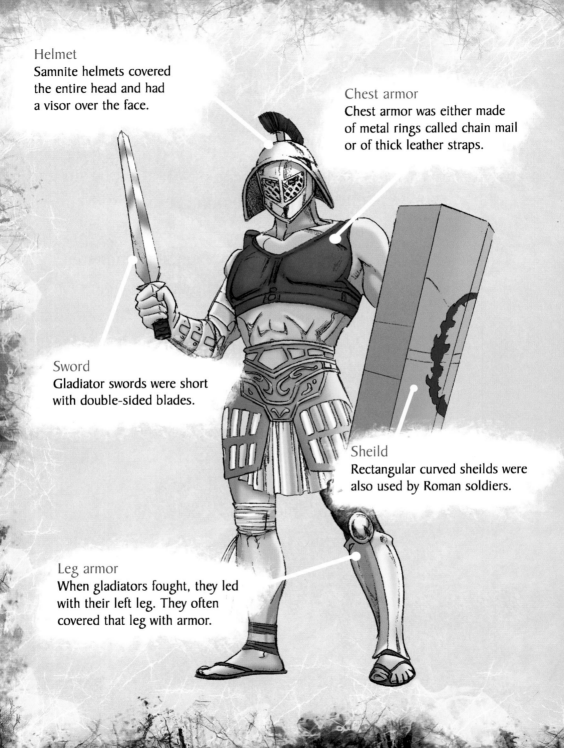

Helmet
Samnite helmets covered the entire head and had a visor over the face.

Chest armor
Chest armor was either made of metal rings called chain mail or of thick leather straps.

Sword
Gladiator swords were short with double-sided blades.

Sheild
Rectangular curved sheilds were also used by Roman soldiers.

Leg armor
When gladiators fought, they led with their left leg. They often covered that leg with armor.

THE MOST FAMOUS GLADIATOR

Spartacus is the most famous gladiator who ever lived. A man of great strength, he was also a natural leader. In 73 BC, he led 70 other enslaved gladiators in an escape from a training school. They started a revolt that attracted thousands of slaves. Spartacus' army defeated the Roman army several times before he was killed in a battle.

The story of Spartacus has inspired authors and movie producers. Actor Kirk Douglas played him in a 1960 film.

CHAPTER IV

THE END OF THE GLADIATORS

LEARN ABOUT
- *The Colosseum*
- *Gladiator battles*
- *Christianity and the Romans*

Gladiator fights were sometimes held outdoors in fenced arenas.

Gladiator games became most popular after AD 80. That year, a huge building called the Flavian Amphitheater opened in Rome. It later became known as the Colosseum. The Colosseum held up to 50,000 people. Thousands of gladiators died fighting in its arena over the next several hundred years. Part of this famous building still stands in Rome today.

GLADIATOR BATTLEFIELDS

Gladiators usually fought each other one on one. But spectators were easily bored. Eventually, gladiators fought in groups of hundreds or even thousands. They hacked and stabbed at each other in huge bloody battles.

The emperor Constantine began the process of eliminating deadly games.

A CHRISTIAN EMPEROR

Gladiators were popular until at least AD 300. In AD 306, Constantine the Great came to power. He was Rome's first Christian emperor.

Before Constantine's rule, Christians were treated with cruelty. They were often thrown into the arena to be eaten by wild animals. In AD 325, Constantine spoke out against violence in the arena. His views began to slowly change public opinion.

Despite Constantine's disapproval, gladiators continued fighting. Romans were used to being entertained by death. Many were unwilling to give up that pleasure.

EDGE FACT

Most Romans did not care what gods people worshipped, as long as they included Roman gods. Christians were disliked because they believed in only one god.

BANNING THE GAMES

As more Romans became Christians, more people tried to stop the violent gladiator games. In AD 404, a Christian monk named Telemachus tried to break up a battle between two gladiators. The crowd was so upset, they beat him to death.

Gladiator games did not officially end until AD 440. The Roman Empire was changing and so were the values of its people. The sport of men killing each other for the amusement of others was finally over.

Over time, the Roman Empire crumbled, and so did the Colosseum.

GLOSSARY

amphitheater (AM-fi-thee-uh-tuhr)—a large, open-air building with rows of seats in a high circle around an arena; in ancient Roman times, gladiators often fought in amphitheaters.

arena (uh-REE-nuh)—a large area that is used for sports or entertainment

empire (EM-pire)—a group of countries that have the same ruler

lanista (lah-NISS-tuh)—a person who owned and trained gladiators

retiarius (ret-ee-AIR-ee-uhss)—a gladiator armed with a net and trident

trident (TRY-dent)—a long spear with three sharp points at its end

READ MORE

Frew, Katherine. *Gladiators: Battling in the Arena.* Way of the Warrior. New York: Children's Press, 2005.

Malam, John. *Gladiators: Life and Death in Ancient Rome.* DK Secret Worlds. New York: DK Publishing, 2002.

INTERNET SITES

FactHound offers a safe, fun way to find Internet sites related to this book. All of the sites on FactHound have been researched by our staff.

Here's how:

1. Visit *www.facthound.com*

2. Choose your grade level.

3. Type in this book ID **0736864296** for age-appropriate sites. You may also browse subjects by clicking on letters, or by clicking on pictures and words.

4. Click on the **Fetch It** button.

FactHound will fetch the best sites for you!

INDEX